WRITE LIKE

WRITING
TO
PERSUADE

CHRIS NOLAN AND LAUREN SPENCER

rosen publishing's
rosen
central®

New York

Published in 2012 by The Rosen Publishing Group, Inc.
29 East 21st Street, New York, NY 10010

Library of Congress Cataloging-in-Publication Data

Nolan, Chris, 1978–
Writing to persuade/Chris Nolan, Lauren Spencer.—1st ed.
    p. cm.—(Write like a pro)
Includes bibliographical references and index.
ISBN 978-1-4488-4685-6 (lib. bdg.)—ISBN 978-1-4488-4691-7 (pbk.)—
ISBN 978-1-4488-4749-5 (6-pack)
1. Composition (Language arts)—Juvenile literature. 2. English language—
Paragraphs—Juvenile literature. 3. Persuasion (Rhetoric)—Juvenile
literature. I. Spencer, Lauren. II. Title.
LB1576.N8255 2012
808'.042—dc22

2011000304

Manufactured in the United States of America

CPSIA Compliance Information: Batch #S11YA: For further information, contact Rosen Publishing, New York, New York, at 1-800-237-9932.

CONTENTS

INTRODUCTION

Persuasive writing introduces an author's strong opinions regarding a specific subject he or she has chosen to write about. When you are writing persuasively about something, your goal is to convince the reader that your opinion is relevant. You do this by using language that conveys balanced thoughts, strong convictions, and respect for the reader.

Persuasive pieces often use emotional subject matter that is based on a personal opinion, such as a letter written to another person describing something the author feels strongly about. Reviews

are a form of persuasive writing. They are meant to convince a reader whether it is a good idea to experience whatever is being reviewed. Writing that argues a specific point can often be found on the editorial page of a newspaper. This type of writing generally focuses on topics for which there are many different opinions and possible arguments.

When writing to persuade, it is crucial that your thoughts be explained clearly and that your opinions be supported by facts. In some cases, detailed research will be required to support your opinions fully. In other cases, your writing will rely more on your own personal beliefs. Since persuasive writing cannot succeed without an audience, respect for the reader is an absolute requirement.

In this book, we will explore various methods for focusing on, investigating, organizing, and writing about a topic so that you can explain your opinions in a convincing manner. We will investigate ways to involve the audience and make your writing more exciting by using figurative language, such as similes, metaphors, hyperbole, and personification. Anecdotes and rhetorical questions are other devices that make persuasive pieces more expressive. We will find ways to define opinions with passion and style—two important elements of any persuasive writing piece.

We will also consider the new technologies for creating and distributing content, such as blogs, wikis, messaging, and social networks, among others. One of the most important considerations to take when using technology to write is to remember whom your audience is. The language you use when sending a text message to a friend will be a lot different than your tone when writing an academic paper. Yet, since we are growing so used to using the text message digital shorthand, it's easy to forget that it may not be appropriate to use texting shorthand in academic papers.

chapter 1

Before You Write

When you are writing persuasively, your goal is to convince the reader of your point of view. By expressing your opinion, which is based on feelings but supported by facts, your audience reads your interpretation of a specific subject or event. The difference between writing subjectively (when you express only feelings) and objectively (when you present only facts) is the difference between persuasive and informative writing. In informative writing, the author generally avoids expressing strong feelings. In persuasive pieces, the author's feelings take center stage. These feelings and opinions, when supported by research, are used to influence a reader's attitude toward the subject.

As you are expressing your opinions, keep your audience in mind. Although you want to convince people of your point of view, you do not want them to feel

ESSENTIAL STEPS

Read and understand different persuasive writing styles, such as the newspaper's editorial section, or a book or movie review.

Choose a persuasive topic.

Explore powers of opinion.

Before you write, make notes on your subject and your audience. You can then work from there on fleshing out what you want to say.

as if you're lecturing them or telling them how to feel. Let readers "see" your point of view, and then they can make up their own minds. In doing so, you avoid talking down to your audience while encouraging them to think for themselves.

Persuasive pieces can be written in several different formats. You may choose to write a persuasive letter to someone about your opinion on a specific topic. Reviews are another form of persuasive writing. These short pieces express your feelings about something specific, such as a book or movie. Your aim is to convince readers whether they should try it. You can review anything: art, literature, food, and many other subjects.

Writing that takes a specific side on an issue where there may be existing disagreement or controversy is known as an argument piece. Although an argument piece may involve a less personal topic than a persuasive essay, it needs to be just as strong. In an argument piece, you need to recognize the opposing view while supporting your opinion with facts.

Understanding Your Point of View

Persuasive writing is usually written in the first person, which means a first-person pronoun such as "I" is used throughout the piece. Persuasive writing is also often written in the present tense. This allows the reader to become involved in the topic, seeing the issue through the author's eyes. If you feel strongly about your subject, your beliefs will come through in your writing.

As you think about possible topics, always keep your reader in mind. Make sure you can communicate to this person the importance of your subject. You want the audience to have every reason to believe as strongly in the topic as you do. Address the reader as "you," and treat him or her the way you would a friend with whom you want to share valuable information. By using a confident tone in your writing, which is your personality and author's "voice," you'll convey how strongly you believe in your cause. It takes logic, organization, and patience, but eventually your point will be clear enough for your reader to decide whether he or she has been persuaded.

What to Write About

Since it's crucial that you care about the topic you choose, take some time to reflect on your options. On a blank sheet of paper, make a list of things that you feel strongly about. The list can include topics such as "Schools should offer wireless Internet access in every classroom" or something on a larger scale that you've thought about for a while, such as "No homework should be given on weekends."

An easy way to get all your ideas on paper is to choose a few topics about different aspects of your life. Think of issues you deal with at home, at school, and while you're with friends. Once you've written down several ideas, return to each topic and list the reasons you feel strongly about each statement. When you find a subject that you have many opinions about, it's a safe bet that this could become your topic. If you have a couple of choices, ask other people's views on each statement. Their answers may help you form a stronger opinion.

In order to firm up your opinions on any topic, put together a graphic organizer called a pro-and-con list. Example:

Computers with wireless Internet access in every classroom

PROS	CONS
Students can do more research in class	Students might be distracted from class work
Teachers can use examples from the Internet	Students might use the Internet to cheat
Interactive projects can be done right in the classroom	Students might visit non-productive Web sites

When constructing your pro-and-con list, take the reasons from your list and make them the examples that appear in each column, either supporting (pro) or arguing against (con) your topic. Your reader will appreciate that both sides of the topic are presented. This will show you've taken the time to look at the issue from different viewpoints. This is why writing a pro-and-con list will expand your opinion and improve your piece.

Exercise: Write It

Think of a past vacation or day trip that was a disaster and write two paragraphs about it. The first paragraph must be completely factual. Use the four

W's: Who went? Where did you travel? When did you go? Why did you go? Consider only facts, such as "Mom and Dad both had time off from work, and I didn't have school." What happened? Again, write only about facts, such as "We boarded an airplane for a twelve-hour flight."

In the second paragraph, write your personal opinions to describe how you felt about the experience. Use ample details to describe your feelings surrounding the trip and what happened during your stay. When you are finished writing, reread both paragraphs. Which one do you like best? Which one has more personality?

Opinions vs. Facts

An opinion is a belief about something that is neither true nor false because it is a personal and subjective feeling. Facts refer to things that actually exist or have happened; therefore, they can be proven true. For example: "There is wireless Internet access at school" is a fact, while the statement "The speed of the wireless Internet access isn't any good" is an opinion.

A Closer Look at Your Opinion Statement

After you have formed an opinion statement and made a pro-and-con list, the time has come to think logically about your viewpoint. It is now time to judge, evaluate, and prove your opinion statement with relevant facts.

This factual information can be gleaned by doing research related to your topic. Be careful, however. If you have chosen an opinion that is too general such as "All Internet access in schools is useful," you might have difficulty proving your point. Avoid using words in your opinion statement that are too strongly aligned with or opposed to any argument. Words that are commonly too positive or too negative to use as part of an opinion statement include "all," "every," "never," "none," "best," and "worst." If your opinion statement uses any of these words, it might be impossible to support with fact-based research.

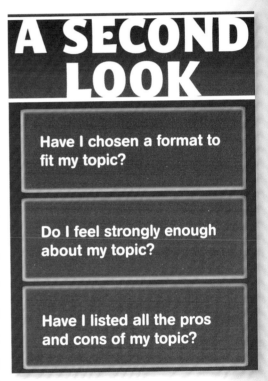

A SECOND LOOK

Have I chosen a format to fit my topic?

Do I feel strongly enough about my topic?

Have I listed all the pros and cons of my topic?

chapter 2

Organizing Your Research

Before you gather the factual information you'll use to support your opinion statement, decide how you want to organize your topic. Because you are presenting how you feel about a specific subject, arrange your points in the order you feel they are most effective. By prioritizing your facts and ideas, you'll be able to take your reader through your thought process in stages. If you build your opinion gradually, the reader will be able to gain a clear and thorough understanding of your opinion. Sometimes writers begin with their least important points and build arguments that are more convincing later. In other cases, this order can be reversed. Writers may begin by starting the piece with their most important and dramatic evidence and following with supporting fact.

Think of at least three points that will support your opinion.

ESSENTIAL STEPS

Organize your thoughts.

Outline your idea.

Research facts to support your opinion.

These ideas will serve as the foundation for your outline. If your persuasive topic is "Hip-hop music is here to stay," your three supporting points might be "Hip-hop is popular"; "Hip-hop is the voice of a generation"; and "Hip-hop is the future of popular music." Writing your persuasive piece in this direction is a little like a fireworks display: it begins with a bang and then builds to a great crescendo.

Using an outline to organize your research can help you establish a clear idea of what you want to say.

Next, you need to create an outline. There are two types of outlines. A topic outline is organized with a list of words or phrases. This type of outline is most often used for shorter essays. A sentence outline organizes the ideas in complete thoughts, so more information can be included.

Longer reports and research papers usually require sentence outlines. With either type of outline, you want to make sure that you include enough information so that you can pick up the thought and expand on it. Be very specific in your outline by focusing on one thought at a time. Example:

Topic Outline

Topic: Hip-hop music is here to stay.
Popular
CD and concert sales high
People watch videos/copy hip-hop styles
Hip-hop influences other art forms
Voice of a generation
Authentic performers
Performers can relate to audience
Respect for audience
Future of popular music
Emerging artists
Critical praise
Hip-hop music evolves

Sentence Outline

Topic: Hip-hop music is here to stay.
Hip-hop is very popular.
Hip-hop music and concert sales are higher than most other styles of music.
Hip-hop artists often start fashion trends.
Hip-hop style and fashion have influenced other art forms, such as movies.
Hip-hop is the voice of a generation.
Hip-hop performers are authentic in their words and dress.

Hip-hop performers can relate to their audience.
Hip-hop artists respect their audience based on their lyrics.
The future of hip-hop is strong.
New hip-hop artists are constantly emerging.
Hip-hop artists have received continuous critical praise.
Hip-hop music is constantly changing to include new sounds and trends.

Backing Up Your Opinion

A well-written persuasive piece requires factual support. By doing sufficient research on your subject, you can find factual information such as statistics, sales records, charts, and graphs and combine that data with other people's critical opinions. Sometimes when you find an opposing viewpoint, you can use it to strengthen your idea by explaining why you don't agree. When you take this approach, stay focused on why you feel strongly about your viewpoint. Avoid criticizing the other person's opinion or being disrespectful in your writing.

To find factual details, reference sources such as encyclopedias contain information you can use to support your subject. For instance, if you need to find the date that the term "hip-hop" was first used, an online encyclopedia dealing with current music will have that data. Magazines, newspapers, and Web sites

Convince your readers by backing up your facts. However, make sure you use reputable resources, such as encyclopedias.

often supply information that includes more opinion-based material.

These sources can be invaluable, since your persuasive piece will be stronger if you can cite someone else who backs up your opinion. Citing a critical opinion, or one given by a person who is respected as an authority in a related field, is also useful if you need to prove a point by argument. If you use any of the information word-for-word from one of your research sources, you must also include the name of that source in your piece. This way, you won't be accused of plagiarism, which is a very serious charge. Example:

In the November 2002 issue of *The Source* magazine, editor in chief David Mays said, "Hip-hop is the voice of a generation."

It's important that what David Mays actually said is surrounded by quotation marks and that you also credit the magazine where you found the quote. You can also paraphrase a comment, which means you give credit to the source while rearranging the words so that you don't need to use quote marks. Example:

When David Mays mentioned long ago in the November 2002 issue of *The Source* magazine that he thought hip-hop was the voice of a generation, I thought he made a great point that is still true today nearly a decade later.

Your Sources

The key to a successful persuasive piece is the ability to gain access to a variety of facts and opinions and use them effectively. This means using the information from your outline to give you the direction to find facts or ideas to include in your writing. As you locate various facts and opinions, write them down. You can do this on the outline itself or by creating a reference chart. For a chart, make two columns on the page. In the first column, copy all the points from your outline. In the second column, note where you found those facts and opinions. If at certain times during your writing you need to refresh your memory or

Outline Facts	Sources
Digital music sales high	*New York Times*, April 15, 2010
Concerts sell out	*New York Times*, April 15, 2010
People watch music videos/copy style	*The Source* magazine, January 2008
Performers authentic	*Vibe* magazine, November 2007
Performers can relate	*Vibe* magazine, November 2007
Respect for community	Youth in Action, online site
New artists	*The Source* magazine, January 2006
Critics wrong	*New York Times*, January 12, 2004
Changes in sound	*Rolling Stone* magazine, September 13, 2004

find a similar fact, you can look to your chart for the original source.

Organizing your sources before you begin writing is helpful because it allows you to focus primarily on writing about your opinions, the true nature of persuasive writing. The purpose of your research is to effectively support your views on the topic.

If you are writing a review, be sure that you have your sources handy, whether that is the book you read, CD you listened to, or the notes you took during the event. With all this information to back you up, you can let your opinions loose on the page in an organized and convincing manner.

A SECOND LOOK

Is my information clearly organized?

Are there enough facts to support my opinion, or do I need to conduct additional research?

Have I recorded my sources accurately?

chapter 3

The First Draft

As we have learned, the main objective of persuasive writing is to convince the reader of your opinion. While you're expecting the readers to make their own decisions about the subject, your goal is to help them see things your way. To do this, you need to be confident of your author's voice, or the tone and style of your writing. The author's voice is meant to appeal to, interest, and persuade your reader. Quite often teachers will say, "Write like you speak," and while that is often true in persuasive writing, you want to make sure that you use language that is clear. This will make it easier for the reader to see your point of view.

ESSENTIAL STEPS

Focus your point of view and zero in on your author's voice.

Apply different writing transitions and techniques.

Write your first draft.

If you are a person who likes to present his or her opinions in a formal way, that style will come through in your piece. If a conversational style is more to your liking, focus your writing in that way. Never insult your reader or suggest that he or she would be foolish not to see the issue as you do. Persuasive writing is meant to point out a certain opinion that is supported by facts. Once you've presented your idea, it is up to readers to make their own decisions.

Transitioning to the Next Idea or Topic

In a persuasive story, the way you present your thoughts is very important. If your sentences are not well connected, your readers will be confused. Transitional words and phrases help ensure a smooth ride for the reader. Phrases such as "therefore," "in fact," and "for this reason" will connect your thoughts in an authoritative way. When writing to persuade, remember to include the opposing point of view in a positive light. This will show that, although you recognize the other side of the issue, your opinion still makes the most sense.

Reviews

A review, whether of a book, a movie, or an event, is a special type of persuasive writing. It expresses to the reader your opinion about what you read or saw without giving any surprises away. It is also important in any type of review to mention the title of the piece and the person who created it at the beginning.

Reviews of art or restaurants also require the writer to be very clear about what is being experienced. The more facts you present at the beginning, the more freedom you have to write about how you feel. This information should help persuade your reader. Don't assume that he or she has any knowledge about your topic. Take readers on a journey into the experience by using descriptive elements. Consider how the experience made you see, hear, smell, taste, and touch like never before, and use descriptive details to provoke those senses.

Your Writing Style

With any effective writing, the use of figurative language and other literary techniques will add style while capturing a reader's attention. Here are some figurative language tools that can add personality to your writing:

Anecdote: A short and interesting story drawn from life that is used to make a point.

Example: When I saw a performance of *Cat on a Hot Tin Roof* at our school, it brought back good memories of when I first saw it years ago with my parents on Broadway.

Rhetorical Question: The word "rhetoric" means to use words effectively. A rhetorical question is one posed for effect. When posing a rhetorical question, no answer is expected. A rhetorical question involves the reader directly.

Example: How do the performers in the school play remember all their lines night after night?

Emotive Language: This is when drama is used to evoke strong feelings from the reader.

Example: Imagine being surrounded by the powerful voices of the most talented students that the school has to offer.

Hyperbole: Exaggeration adds effect to further make the point.

Example: Imagine being surrounded by the most amazing school singing voices that the world has ever heard.

Parallel: When you point out both sides of the issue, you are using a parallel.

Example: To be swept away by talent is wonderful; to be swept out of the door by a bad performance is painful.

Figurative Language: Using similes, metaphors, and personification to bring your persuasive writing to life.

Example: (Simile) When the members of the choral group sang, their voices lit up the stage like fireworks. (Metaphor) They made an explosion of sound. (Personification) Their microphones practically danced across the stage.

Putting Pen to Paper

As you begin writing your first draft, refer to your outline and research. Make sure that you have some uninterrupted time so that you can get all your thoughts on the page without stopping.

Your opening sentence or paragraph must capture the reader's attention by involving him or her in your topic. To accomplish this, address your audience directly by using "you" or "we." Also, appeal to the reader's sense of excitement by enticing him or her into the topic with an anecdote or fact. There is no need to state what is already obvious, such as "A school talent show is a big event." Instead, begin with a statement about talent shows that will immediately resonate with a reader.

Make sure you're fully prepared with your outline and your research before you actually begin writing. That will make the process run much more smoothly.

When presenting your point of view, be sure you are reasonable. Since persuasive writing is meant to convince the reader of something he or she may not agree with or be aware of, take your time in explaining why you feel the way you do. Although confidence is an important element in persuasive writing, avoid boasting or bragging. This approach will often turn the reader off both the subject and the writer. Support your claims with well-researched facts. The order in which you present your information often means the difference between convincing the reader or just capturing his or her interest. Writing about your topic in a systematic manner will let the reader know that you have taken the time to support your opinions fully.

The final paragraph of your persuasive piece is extremely important. This is the last chance you have to state your opinion. Your goal is to leave the reader with a strong sense of why he or she should consider your viewpoint. To do this,

A SECOND LOOK

Does my author's voice come through clearly?

Is my opinion strongly stated?

Do I stick to the point?

Did I use literary techniques to bring my first draft to life?

restate your original opinion in a new way. Decide exactly what you would like the reader to remember about your topic. If it makes sense and isn't too dramatic, end with a personal appeal, such as "I recommend strongly that you not miss this year's school talent show." Example:

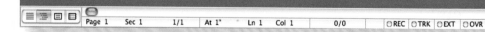

Document1

School Hullabaloo

This year's talent show was right on.

The first performer was Tracy Warner, and she moved me with a rendition of "Girls Just Want to Have Fun." It was phenomenal. Her voice shook the building like an earthquake.

After Greg Epson's group, the Crimsons, belted out four rap-metal tunes, there was a short intermission. The second half was just as excellent as the first.

What impressed me the most was the composure of each performer. It reminded me of the time I watched *American Idol* being taped, and the singers acted as if they'd been performing all their lives. If you go to see only one school production this year, make it this one. You won't be sorry!

Page 1 Sec 1 1/1 At 1" Ln 1 Col 1 0/0 ○REC ○TRK ○EXT ○OVR

chapter 4

The Revision Process

Revision is the act of reexamining and improving your writing. Revising does not mean correcting spelling and punctuation, which will come later. Revising means to investigate your draft and make sure the ideas flow in an organized and logical manner and that the language you've used will hold the reader's interest.

With a red pen in hand—or any color that stands out on the page—start your revision by examining your writing for areas where you can cut unnecessary or repeated information. Avoid writing that rambles on and fails to make its point. Next, read through the piece to make sure that the order of sentences flows and supports your main opinion. Check to ensure you've answered any questions that your reader might have about

ESSENTIAL STEPS

Read over your first draft, making edits and changes wherever necessary.

Check that statements and facts are presented clearly.

Make sure that your facts are presented in a convincing manner.

Polish your sentence structure. Look for and omit repeated or unnecessary information.

All writing needs revising. This involves making sure your arguments are clear and supported by facts. It also entails correcting spelling and grammar.

the topic and that your ideas are supported by facts. Look for loose ends and tie them up by elaborating, rewriting, or adding details to support your main idea. Finally, make sure that the language you are using expresses your enthusiasm for your subject. Look for places where you can express strong emotion. As you check for these elements, make changes directly on the page.

Make It Clear

Since your persuasive piece ultimately depends on your ability to deliver a strong opinion, you must make sure that your subject has been presented clearly. Doing this will ensure that the reader understands your message without becoming confused. As you revise your first draft, make sure that all of your opinions are supported by facts. When a statement is made that is not supported, it can confuse the reader.

Here are some examples of unclear writing:

Example:

This sentence jumps to a conclusion. The statement "Wearing school uniforms saves lives" is an exaggeration, since there is no proof that it is true. By adding a qualifier such as "in my opinion" at the beginning and then continuing to explain why you feel so strongly about this statement, you will impress upon the reader that this is your opinion.

Example:

The statement "Students never fight over school uniforms" sets up a situation that makes school uniforms seem more powerful than they are. Soften the statement by using factual support: "In my research, I've found that students almost never fight over school uniforms, whereas without uniforms..."

Example:

The sentence "In schools where there are no uniforms, fights break out every day" contains an exaggerated half-truth. By showing that there is less fighting in schools where uniforms are required, the point would be delivered in a more convincing way: "Last year, Morris School had twice as many fights over clothing worn at the school than Bellmore, where the students wear uniforms."

Example:

The sentence "School uniforms are perfect because everyone likes them" suggests that because "everyone" likes school uniforms, they are good. Just because many people like something doesn't necessarily mean it's a good thing. If you want to make a similar point, take a poll or do a study of some sort and use the results for your piece: "Sixty-eight percent of those students asked said that they thought school uniforms eliminated some tensions between students. It seems that more people like them than not."

Example:

The statement "School uniforms are like the outfits astronauts wear in space" is incomplete because it compares two things that are not similar. If the sentence is used as a comparison, you must back it up with a reason: "School uniforms are like the outfits astronauts wear in outer space because students are also constantly exploring new territory."

Sentence Structure

Because you don't want the reader to be distracted from your persuasive opinion by choppy or otherwise poor sentence structure, make sure that your piece includes complete, informative sentences. The types of sentences that will make your opinion felt most strongly are declarative, imperative, and exclamatory. Also, a mix of complex and compound sentences will give your writing more variety. Example: Here is a letter written to persuade the school superintendent about why school uniforms are worthwhile.

Document1

November 7, 2010
14 Somewhere Rd.
Thistown, Somestate 55535

Dr. Jane Anderson
Superintendent of Schools
Thistown, Somestate 55535

Dear Dr. Anderson:

During lunch with my classmates the other day, the subject turned to school uniforms. My name is Sally Clipper, and I attend Bellmore School. It is an excellent school, and it has gotten even better in the last two years since we've had mandatory school uniforms. Before students wore uniforms, there were always fights over someone taking someone else's jacket or hat. There was a lot of attitude from one student to another about who was wearing the latest fashions and who was cool or not based on what he or she was wearing. Because our school doesn't have these problems, we can now focus on educating our minds.

When I read in our local paper that you were thinking of reversing the uniform policy in our school, I decided I had to write and let you know how I feel. I also thought it would be helpful if I took a student poll so that you could see how others feel about this decision. On Tuesday of last week, I asked students, teachers, and parents about school uniforms. This is what I found out: 73 percent felt that uniforms were a good thing; 17 percent

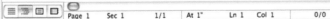

Page 1   Sec 1   1/1   At 1"   Ln 1   Col 1   0/0

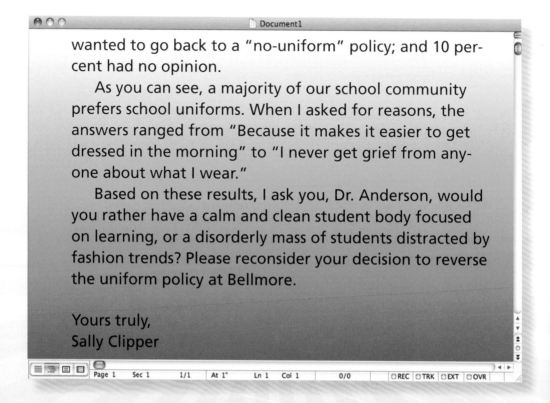

wanted to go back to a "no-uniform" policy; and 10 per-cent had no opinion.

As you can see, a majority of our school community prefers school uniforms. When I asked for reasons, the answers ranged from "Because it makes it easier to get dressed in the morning" to "I never get grief from any-one about what I wear."

Based on these results, I ask you, Dr. Anderson, would you rather have a calm and clean student body focused on learning, or a disorderly mass of students distracted by fashion trends? Please reconsider your decision to reverse the uniform policy at Bellmore.

Yours truly,
Sally Clipper

Types of Sentences

Declarative Sentence: A declarative sentence makes a statement about a person, place, thing, or idea.

Example: Our school uniforms are blue-and-yellow-checked skirts for the girls, blue pants for the boys, and white shirts for everybody.

Imperative Sentence: The point of an imperative sentence is to give a command. It is aimed directly at the reader.

Example: Consider all the money saved on clothes when students wear uniforms to school instead of traditional clothing.

Exclamatory Sentence: A strong emotion or surprise is expressed in an exclamatory sentence and is usually followed by an explanation point.

Example: It would be great never to have to worry about what to wear!

Complex Sentence: When you put a dependent clause—so-called because it can't exist alone—into a complete sentence, it makes a complex sentence.

Example: The student uniforms, which include our school colors, look great during athletic events and pep rallies. While the sentence "The student uniforms look great during athletic events and pep rallies" is complete on its own, adding the dependent clause "which include our school colors" adds a detail that gives the reader more information.

Compound Sentence: Taking two complete sentences—sentences that have a subject and a verb and can stand on their own—and joining them creates a compound sentence. You can accomplish this by using a semicolon or conjunction, which is a word used to join sentence elements. Words like "and," "or," and "but" are conjunctions.

Examples: School uniforms look crisp and neat on the first day of class; you have to clean them every day in order to keep them that way.

Or you can use a conjunction:

School uniforms look crisp and neat on the first day of class, but you have to clean them every day in order to keep them that way.

Now that you have begun the revision process and have checked your writing for its sentence structure and overall clarity, it is also a good time to examine its ratio of facts to opinions. Make sure that each strong opinion is supported by one or more factual statements, and that your research has been properly cited throughout your work. You can always refer to your reference chart if you neglected to include this information earlier. In addition, examine your writing line by line for awkward phrasing, incomplete or unclear thoughts, or arguments that seem illogical.

Since a persuasive piece is one that contains emotion, it is a good idea to read it aloud to check if the powers of persuasion really work. A great way to find this out is to switch papers with a partner and have him or her read it to you. Are you convinced? Make a copy for yourself so that you can keep notes about where you can make useful changes.

The Art of Letter Writing

After getting permission from a principal or teacher, choose someone in the public eye—such as a celebrity, a politician, or an athlete—and write a persuasive letter to that person explaining all of the reasons he or she should come to your school to speak to students on career day.

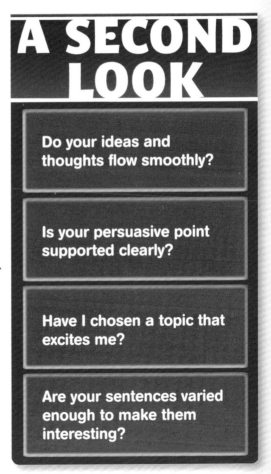

A SECOND LOOK

Do your ideas and thoughts flow smoothly?

Is your persuasive point supported clearly?

Have I chosen a topic that excites me?

Are your sentences varied enough to make them interesting?

chapter 5

Making It Look Professional: Proofreading and Editing

When you are writing to persuade your reader, your title will need to reflect your main point. For instance, if you are writing a review, the title should refer to the item being reviewed without giving away details about the film, book, or show. The title should serve as an invitation to read the piece or attend the performance because it contains just enough information to lure the reader by making him or her curious. For opinion pieces, an exclamatory title helps catch a reader's attention. Keep it short and to the point.

Rhetorical questions can also work to draw in an audience. If you've written a persuasive letter, no title is necessary. However, you do need to make sure that you have a heading that includes the correct address and names, and that you've added the date.

ESSENTIAL STEPS

Add an informative title that illustrates your main point.

Complete a spelling and grammar check.

Get feedback from others

Once you have chosen a title, examine your writing for spelling and punctuation errors. If you've written your piece on a computer, now is a good time to use the spell-check function.

For handwritten stories, use your dictionary to look up words that don't seem correct. At this stage, you probably feel that you know the piece well, but pretend you are reading it for the first time. This will help you catch places where grammar, spelling, or clarity need to be improved. Often, your computer's spell-check function will catch grammatical mistakes, but you also need to be on the lookout for clunky sentences, missed commas, improper punctuation, or any other errors.

Verb Agreement

So that the effect of your persuasive argument is fully felt, make sure that any confusion in the writing is clarified. Verb tense agreement is important, so in this final proofreading stage, examine your verbs very carefully. Make sure that tenses match from the beginning to the end of your piece. If your persuasive writing has to do with a current situation, it needs to be written in the present tense. If you are referring to something that has happened before, use the past tense; and if you're focusing on an issue yet to happen, the future tense is the way to go.

To ensure that your piece has the correct focus and sets the proper tone to be thoroughly convincing, set it aside for a day and then reread it with "fresh" eyes. Another idea is to enlist the help of a partner for a final read-through. Have your partner read your story to reexamine its basic elements. Use the following list to refresh your memory:

- Can short sentences be combined to make them more interesting?
- Should longer sentences be divided into two more powerful and precise thoughts?
- Consider adding a rhetorical question or exclamation to add impact.
- Are the transitions from paragraph to paragraph smooth?
- Does each paragraph focus on one specific point?
- Do all the sentences in the paragraph support the main point?
- Do the sentences flow in a logical order?

The Right Editor for You

An editor is someone who can help you shape your writing. He or she will offer suggestions and point out areas that need improvement. Especially with persuasive pieces, the full impact of your writing can only be felt if it is noticed by others. When revising your final document, you should avoid rewriting it completely. You should instead focus on specific areas that need improvement. This is where an editor or a writing partner will come in handy.

An editor's job is to act as an unbiased reader to help you improve your writing. Editors offer suggestions or point out issues that you may have overlooked.

When choosing an editor, it is best to not depend on someone who knows you too well. In that case, he or she probably thinks that everything you do is wonderful or may be nervous about hurting your feelings. The idea is to have a critical review to make sure that your writing is clear and persuasive.

There are many ways that you can work with an editor to improve your writing. While he or she reads the piece, watch his or her facial expressions. Ask questions about his or her reaction. Get out your notes and correct any rough patches. Another angle is to read your piece during an informal gathering to get a group's reaction. Hand out a sheet with some questions pertaining to the piece, and have your listeners fill out your survey after you've finished. Tell them they don't need to put their names on it, but only answer the questions honestly.

Example Questionnaire

- List three reasons why this piece was convincing.
- Which statement stood out the most?
- Was any information unclear, and therefore not persuasive?

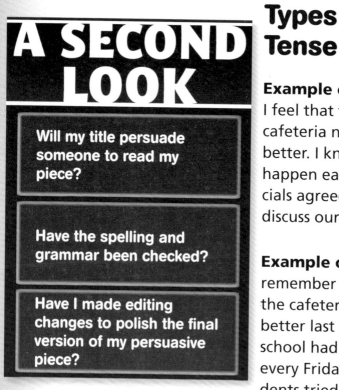

A SECOND LOOK

Will my title persuade someone to read my piece?

Have the spelling and grammar been checked?

Have I made editing changes to polish the final version of my persuasive piece?

Types of Verb Tense

Example of Present Tense: I feel that the food in the cafeteria needs to be much better. I know that this could happen easily if school officials agreed to sit down and discuss our menu choices.

Example of Past Tense: I remember that the food in the cafeteria was so much better last year when the school had International Day every Friday and the students tried different foods.

"GOOD TASTE"

It is my opinion that the food in the cafeteria of Millerbrook School could be improved through better food choices. The options offered now by the cafeteria are boring. By offering foods from different regions of the world, students will be exposed to a sampling from a variety of cultures.

While I know that not everyone may like the idea of changing school lunches to include cuisine that they've never heard of, I think that it would be enlightening. I'm not suggesting that the cafeteria entirely do away with standard fare, but why not add more variety? Along with the daily choices, include an Indian curry dish or Mexican enchiladas.

I have talked with students from other schools who are offered a variety of food choices, so I know that it's possible. I also know that kosher and vegetarian food is available in our cafeteria for some students, but why isn't it available to everyone?

You might be asking, "But how will the cooks ever find those recipes?" Well, here is my answer: hold a contest! In the school newsletter, there could be an invitation to submit favorite family recipes. This way, Millerbrook students would have a chance to try foods from many lands. I feel that this would be a great learning experience.

Example of Future Tense: The food in the cafeteria will improve if school officials take some time to determine what students like to eat and what is healthy for them.

PROOFREADING

Here are the symbols that should be used to give instructions for corrections when you or someone else is correcting your piece:

∧	Insert letters, words, or sentences
ℓ	Delete
⌃	Insert a comma
⌄	Apostrophe or single quotation mark
⌄⌄	Double quotation marks
∿	Transpose elements (switch the order)
#	Insert a space
⌒	Close up this space
⊙	Use a period here
¶	Begin new paragraph
no¶	No paragraph

chapter 6

Presenting Your Writing to an Audience

Now that you've created your persuasive piece, you want to make sure that your final version is presented in a way that will be effective. The words and meaning of a persuasive piece are important, but the form in which it is presented will also have an impact on your reader's interest. The way in which writing is presented has a huge impact on how we respond to it. If you think of almost any product, you'll notice that its packaging makes it more attractive. In writing presentations, this theory also hold true. Since a persuasive piece requires an audience, make sure that it is as inviting to look at as it is convincing to read.

Start with the words. If they are written on a computer, make sure the font style and size are easy to read and the ink color is black. Handwritten pieces should be in blue or black ink, unless you've been

ESSENTIAL STEPS

Put together final draft.

Fine-tune it for presentation.

Look for interesting places to present the piece.

Once your writing is complete, it's time to prepare it for presentation. This involves making sure it's fully edited and formatted properly.

instructed otherwise. Next, think about the form of your persuasive piece.

For a letter, the standard letter format must be used with the date at the top and the correct salutation and address. If you have any questions about these, do a little research and make sure you've got it correct because you'll have a hard time convincing someone if you've misspelled his or her name or sent the letter to the wrong address.

For a review, you might want to use graphics or photographs to enhance the piece. This kind of additional attention can really bring your point to life, especially if you are trying to persuade the reader to take part in whatever activity you're reviewing. There is nothing more helpful than a picture to allow a person to visualize a point of view. If you use a picture that someone else has taken, remember to give that person credit.

If you've written an opinion piece that would best fit into a newspaper, you can print the story in columns. But check first with your teacher to make sure this format is acceptable. Opinion pieces usually stand on their own without any additional graphics because the words carry the whole story.

Last and certainly not least, you must make sure that your name is featured on your story. This is important so that readers can appreciate whose opinion they're reading.

Getting Your Writing Out There

Since the style of persuasive writing is so dependent on the outside world for a response, there are quite a few options for how to present your work. Here are some ideas:

Start a letter-writing campaign about an important issue in your school or community. Gather some persuasive letters and send them to the decision-makers, then see what impact they have. There is always power in numbers, and if your persuasive letters are well presented with a clear message, you can end up making a strong

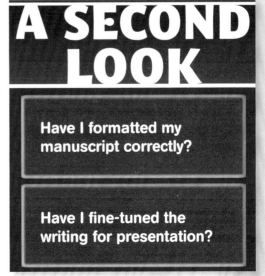

A SECOND LOOK

Have I formatted my manuscript correctly?

Have I fine-tuned the writing for presentation?

impression. At the very least, you should receive a reply as to why the idea is a good one or not.

Talk to your peers, classmates, or teachers about a cause that you feel strongly about. If there are others who feel the same way, consider holding a rally to present your views. Write persuasive speeches (opinion pieces), hang banners with catchy persuasive slogans (sayings with impact), or invite a person from outside (by writing a persuasive letter) who also holds your point of view to be a guest speaker.

Find a local or school paper where you can submit an opinion piece on something you feel strongly about.

Write a persuasive letter to a magazine, newspaper, or television station about something you've seen in its pages or on its network. Explain why you agree or disagree.

As you can tell, there are many reasons to learn to write an effective persuasive article, letter, review, or editorial. If you practice backing up your opinions with appropriate facts, persuasive writing will eventually come naturally.

chapter 7

Persuasive Writing in the Digital Age

The rules of effective writing change little over time. However, the technology we use to create and distribute our writing has evolved greatly over just the past few years. Writing and creating content on an electronic device such as a computer, tablet, or even a phone allows us many conveniences. These include spell-check, grammar check, and predictive text, in which the device predicts the word you wish to write based on the first letters you type. As for distributing that content, the growing popularity of writing platforms has not only changed how we create our content, but also how easily we can send it to our readership.

These technologies may seem completely beneficial on the surface. Yet, there are always trade-offs that come with convenience. Composition tools such as

ESSENTIAL STEPS

Choose which digital platform I'm going to use.

Make sure the writing style is appropriate.

Proofread.

spell-check and predictive text can unintentionally result in bad writing, such as a misused, correctly spelled word, or an unintended word altogether. Distribution tools such as blogs and collaborative documents expose the writer to even greater potential problems because once your writing is in cyberspace, it could be there forever.

Blogs

Blogs are growing in popularity because they're an easy way to publish your writing and distribute it to a wide audience. Blogs also have the added benefit of being social. Readers can comment on the posting or send it to other readers through various means, such as e-mail, Facebook, Twitter, or even their own blogs.

Microblogs are a variety of traditional blogs whose postings and comments tend to be shorter and less formal. Examples of microblogging sites are Twitter and Tumblr.

If you are writing a persuasive piece as a blog post, it is particularly important that you edit and proofread with utmost care. Once the text is in cyberspace, it's difficult if not impossible to take down. Many people have the false impression that a digital posting can be easily edited, revised, updated, or deleted. The opposite is often the case. While you may be able to control your postings if they're in your own blogging account, your text may be copied and redistributed throughout the Web and posted on other servers, in which case you would have no control over the content.

You can also participate in blogs by commenting on other people's posts. It's important, however, to maintain a level of professionalism, called "net etiquette" or "netiquette," when posting comments. Avoid spamming, or posting the same content multiple times on different posts. Also avoid trolling and flaming. Trolling is posting inflammatory off-topic comments on blog postings. Flaming is posting comments that are abusive or hurtful

Wikis

Wikis are information Web sites where users collaborate to create the content. The advantage of wikis is that they tap the knowledge and resources of anyone who wants to participate. And because they are community-based, they are, to a certain degree, self-policing in that incorrect information is often corrected by screeners in the community. However, since professionals are not editing these sites, the information can be unreliable. Wikis should also never be used as an authority for research. They may be a good starting point, but information sources should only be used if they come from a reputable publication whose writers and editors are certified experts.

Messaging

Messaging is informal communication through text messaging, instant messaging and other messaging services, such as Facebook mail. Messaging is usually less formal and quicker than e-mail, lacking a subject line and often going without a greeting or salutation.

Since messages are often written on nontraditional keyboards, such as those on phones, a new language of abbreviations, acronyms, and shorthand has popped up to communicate quickly. It is important to be conscious of who your reader is when messaging. While you may use informal language with friends and family, you should always be professional when messaging in a formal capacity, such as to a potential employer. Use correct spelling and grammar. This is particularly important with e-mail, which is the main form of communication in professional settings.

Collaborative Documents

Collaborative documents are those that are stored on a third-party server and can be shared among a group of people, also known as cloud computing. Cloud computing is the concept of storing all information on a third-party server, the "cloud," which allows you the freedom of not having to worry about losing your documents if your computer crashes or is stolen. However, there are trade-offs to this convenience as well. While your writing is saved on another server, it is out in cyberspace and can potentially be stolen.

Cloud computing also offers the benefit of saving past revisions of a document. Depending on the company that stores these documents, they may exist in cyberspace or on the company's servers forever. This raises the question of who owns the copyright to the content you create. If you write a novel that's hosted on another company's server, does it own the copyright to that content, and should you be concerned if that company is sold or goes out of business?

Also, what if someone steals your content? There are two categories of copyright infringement: direct and indirect. Direct copyright infringement occurs when a person uses copyrighted material in a way that is not allowed. Indirect infringement occurs when you help others copy material that is copyrighted. One common example of indirect infringement is posting serial numbers or "unlock codes" on a Web site so that others can use software that has been copied illegally. Another example is providing software programs that break the copy protection on computer games or movie DVDs. It's illegal and unethical to pass along unlock codes, so don't do it. And don't think it's clever to come up with ways to get around copy protection on computer games—it could get you into a lot of trouble.

The Digital Millennium Copyright Act was passed in 1998. It addresses some of the new copyright infringement issues resulting from the Internet, wireless technology, and recording devices such as CD and DVD writers. Among other things, the law makes it a crime to provide tools to other people that allow them to illegally make copies of copyrighted material. It also provides guidelines and protections for those who have sites on which others post material. The act protects the person or company that owns the Web site from being held responsible if other people illegally post copyrighted material on the site, as long as the Web site's owner follows guidelines outlined in the act.

The companies that provide collaborative document services understand that users are concerned about privacy. Because of this concern, most offer a number of options to protect your documents, such as tiers of privacy and the ability to back them up on your own computer. Even though you may have these options, it's important to be careful when using them.

Always check the privacy settings, as it's easy to mistake a private document for a public one, which could wind up on search engines.

Also, it's a good idea to regularly download and back up your documents on your computer just in case something goes wrong with the hosting company. It's easy to say that these big companies would never lose your documents, but there have been many huge technology companies that have gone out of business and left their users stranded.

Message Boards

Message boards are a great way for a group of people to share their knowledge on a given subject. There's a message board for virtually every topic imaginable, from bicycling to cell phones, football to movies. People often turn to these forums for help answering questions. If you have some expertise on a subject, they're a great way to share your knowledge.

However, as with any community endeavor, there should be a level of netiquette. When posting, make sure you stick to the subject. If you disagree with another poster, do so respectfully and avoid flaming and/or trolling. Remember, what you write online could potentially stay in cyberspace forever.

Social Networks

Social networks are increasingly becoming a cornerstone in our social and professional lives. Therefore, it's important to understand who your audience is before posting content.

Facebook and MySpace are two of the most popular networking sites among teens. You or someone you know probably has created a profile on one, or even both, of these sites. While they can make it easy to connect with your friends, it is important to be careful about whom you contact, and how much information you reveal about yourself. For example, depending on the privacy policy, social networks sometimes automatically make your name, profile photo, friends, and other personal information available to everyone by default.

In the online world, just as in real life, you can choose how much personal information you want to share with others. Would you share personal information such as your address, the name of your school, or your phone number with a stranger?

A SECOND LOOK

Do I understand that my writing will be in cyberspace, potentially forever?

Have I followed the rules of proper netiquette?

You probably learned at a very young age that the answer to this question is "no." If you decide to open a Facebook or MySpace account, it is important to familiarize yourself with the site's privacy settings.

Privacy settings allow you to choose who you want to share your personal information with. You can make your profile private, which means that other online users need your permission to view your personal information. It is safest to let only people you know, such as family members and friends, see your profile.

Even if you don't use your real name online, it's easy to reveal a lot of information—maybe more than you should! Details add up. The name of your school, your age, and what things interest you all point to one person—you! If someone who finds you online can find you in real life, you could put yourself in danger.

GLOSSARY

anecdote A short, entertaining account of an event.

complex sentence A sentence formed by one independent clause and one or more dependent clauses.

compound sentence A sentence in which two independent clauses are joined together with a coordinate conjunction.

conjunction A word used to connect individual words or groups of words.

credit An acknowledgment of work done.

declarative sentence A sentence that makes a strong statement.

dependent clause A clause that cannot stand on its own and thus depends on the rest of a sentence to make sense.

format The style or manner of a piece of writing.

hyperbole Figurative language that uses extreme exaggeration.

independent clause A clause that expresses a complete thought and can stand alone as a sentence.

metaphor A figure of speech that compares two things that are not alike to each other without using "like" or "as."

objective Being without bias or prejudice.

paraphrase To reword something spoken or printed.

personification Using figurative language to give something that is not human lifelike qualities.

perspective A specific point of view when investigating something.

plagiarism Taking someone else's writing and passing it off as one's own.

point of view A perspective; an opinion.

simile A figure of speech that compares two things that are not alike by using "like" or "as."

source The place where information is provided.

subject The topic of a writing piece.

subjective The view of a position resulting from the feeling of a person; personal.

theory The analysis of a set of facts in their relation to one another.

topic The subject of a piece of writing.

topic sentence A sentence that describes what the piece of writing will be about.

transition Tying two ideas together smoothly with a word or phrase.

FOR MORE INFORMATION

National Council of Teachers of English (NCTE)

Achievement Awards in Writing

1111 Kenyon Road

Urbana, IL 61901-1096

Web site: http://www.ncte.org

The National Council of Teachers of English is devoted to improving the teaching and learning of English and the language arts at all levels of education.

National Scholastic Press Association (NSPA)

2221 University Avenue SE, Suite 121

Minneapolis, MN 55414

Web site: http://www.studentpress.org

The National Scholastic Press Association was founded in 1921 and annually hosts high school journalism conventions across the country.

Reading, Writing, and Art Awards

Weekly Reader Corporation

200 First Stamford Place

P.O. Box 120023

Stamford, CT 06912-0023

Web site: http://www.weeklyreader.com

Weekly Reader magazines and digital content provide teachers with a systematic, sequential progression of vocabulary and concept complexity.

Publishing and Posting

Below is a list of publications and Web sites that welcome submissions from young writers.

Figment.com

Web site: http://www.figment.com

E-mail: info@figment.com

Skipping Stones

Multicultural Children's Magazine

P.O. Box 3939

Eugene, OR 97403

Web site: http://www.skippingstones.org

Web Sites

Due to the changing nature of Internet links, Rosen Publishing has developed an online list of Web sites related to the subject of this book. This site is updated regularly. Please use this link to access the list:

http://www.rosenlinks.com/wlp/wtp

FOR FURTHER READING

Caine, Karen. *Writing to Persuade: Minilessons to Help Students Plan, Draft, and Revise, Grades 3-8.* Portsmouth, NH: Heinemann, 2008.

Clark, Roy Peter. *Writing Tools: 50 Essential Strategies for Every Writer.* New York, NY: Little, Brown and Company, 2008.

DiPrince, Dawn, and Cheryl Miller Thurston. *Unjournaling: Daily Writing Exercises That Are Not Personal, Not Introspective, Not Boring!* Waco, TX: Prufrock Press, Inc., 2010.

Dunn, Danielle, and Jessica Dunn. *A Teen's Guide to Getting Published*, revised ed. Waco, TX: Prufrock Press, 2006.

Flash Kids Editors. *Fearless Writing: Essay Workbook* (Flash Kids Fearless). New York, NY: Spark Publishing, 2007.

Flash Kids Editors. *Fearless Writing: Research Paper Workbook* (Flash Kids Fearless). New York, NY: Spark Publishing, 2007.

Fogarty, Mignon. *Grammar Girl's Quick and Dirty Tips for Better Writing* (Quick & Dirty Tips). New York, NY: Henry Holt and Company, 2008.

INDEX

About the Authors

Chris Nolan is a writer living in New York.

Lauren Spencer is originally from California and now lives in New York City, where she teaches writing workshops in public schools. She also writes lifestyle and music articles for magazines.

Photo Credits

Cover Fuse/Getty Images; pp. 4–5 iStockphoto/Thinkstock; p. 8 Flying Colours, Ltd./Photodisc/Thinkstock; p. 15 © Michael Newman/PhotoEdit; p. 18 Courtesy of Encyclopædia Britannica, Inc.; p. 26 Comstock/Thinkstock; p. 30 Shutterstock.com; p. 33 © www.istockphoto.com/Viktoriya Yatskina; pp. 41, 46 © Bob Daemmrich/PhotoEdit; p. 43 © www.istockphoto.com/by_nicholas.

Editor: Nicholas Croce; Photo Researcher: Karen Huang